# SHORT WAL[

## *Dorse[*
## *Pubs*

### Leigh Hatts

COUNTRYSIDE BOOKS
NEWBURY, BERKSHIRE

COUNTRYSIDE BOOKS
3 Catherine Road
Newbury, Berkshire

ISBN 1 85306 335 5

Designed by Mon Mohan
Cover illustration by Colin Doggett
Photographs by the author

Produced through MRM Associates Ltd., Reading
Typeset by The Midlands Book Typesetting Company, Loughborough
Printed and bound by Woolnough Bookbinding Ltd, Irthlingborough

# Contents

## Publisher's Note

We hope that you obtain considerable enjoyment from this book; great care has been taken in its preparation. However, changes of landlord and actual closures are sadly not uncommon. Likewise, although at the time of publication all routes followed public rights of way or permitted paths, diversion orders can be made and permissions withdrawn.

We cannot of course be held responsible for such diversion orders and any inaccuracies in the text which result from these or any other changes to the routes nor any damage which might result from walkers trespassing on private property. However we are anxious that all details covering the walks and the pubs are kept up to date and would therefore welcome information from readers which would be relevant to future editions.

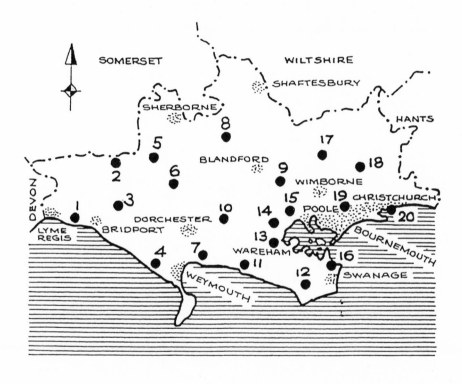

Area map showing locations of the walks.

# Introduction

Dorset is a county of great contrast. Little spoilt and centrally placed Dorchester remains the county town but the majority of the population is to be found in the south-east corner where Poole and the former Hampshire towns of Bournemouth and Christchurch touch each other.

The Dorset coast, arguably the finest of the south-west peninsula, is one of contrast from the low cliff near Mudeford in the east to the highest point on the south coast at Golden Cap in the west. In between are the famous chalk cliffs of the 'Isle' of Purbeck. The Stour Valley runs from the north-east to the far south-east near the precious Dorset heathland, whilst the folds of the west and north Dorset hills hide delightful villages.

Although the growing south-east population has resulted in an impressive choice of thriving pubs in the Wimborne area and the flat countryside north of the Bournemouth conurbation, there are also fine inns away from the urban fringe and in the little populated areas. Many pubs are welcoming freehouses which rarely feature in the standard guide books.

Nationally the number of pubs is declining and those which survive are the ones which have returned to the old tradition of offering good food and a welcome to strangers, rather than just a pint and a pie for regulars. Dorset still has its great county breweries such as Dorchester's Eldridge Pope, Blandford's Hall & Woodhouse and Bridport's Palmers and their tied houses are particularly good. Hall & Woodhouse encourages walkers to use a pub as the base for circular walks. The inn at Spetisbury is already stocking local mineral water to meet the new demand. Now, even in small towns, it is often possible to claim that the best quality and best value lunch is to be found in a pub.

Pubs providing full lunch menus tend not to be open in the afternoon – the need for the traditional staff break before the evening is appreciated even more today. But the trend towards taking advantage of easier opening hours is to be found along the coast in summer with those establishments not advertising all day opening adopting an elastic policy according to the weather. This book lists only firm opening times.

Many of the pubs featured here are near some of Dorset's unique features such as England's smallest church, the mysterious Cerne Giant or a Stour mill and the best way to discover them is on foot. The walks are easy but remember that the countryside is always changing. Sometimes the ground will inevitably be very wet and fields can look very different when crops give way to cattle. Also look out for temporary path diversions which, in Dorset, are always well signposted. A map is a useful companion and readers will find that the OS Purbeck & South Dorset Outdoor Leisure Map is the best map for the south coast.

If you are leaving your car in the pub car park it is advisable to check with the landlord before setting out – normally there will not be any problem.

An enjoyable walk needs not only good countryside but the special view or historic building along with refreshment. The routes suggested in this book lead to rewarding paths and good food.

Leigh Hatts
Spring 1995

# Seatown
# The Anchor Inn

Seatown is the grand name for a fishing hamlet which had a sideline in smuggling. The 'Chideock Gang', controlled by the mysterious 'Colonel', organised pack horses to rush the goods up to Somerset for swift sales. Seatown women had a reputation for being 'pregnant' due to the hiding of casks under their clothes. In the village the tiny river Winniford is still crossed by the packhorse bridge. The Anchor Inn is the centre of Seatown life for fishermen and coastal walkers. In summer they are joined by campers from the holiday park. Since 1986 the inn has had a real anchor outside from the *Hope of Amsterdam*, which foundered off Chesil Beach in January 1748 on its way back from South America, loaded with gold and silver. Every ounce of treasure has long been dug from the pebbles. The inn is tucked under the cliff, just inside the valley entrance – cliff erosion has removed a farm and a coastal road that was between the inn and the sea.

The two small bars are suitably cosy, with small windows to keep out the cold during winter storms and walls which are crowded with fascinating pictures of past times. There is even a framed *Private Eye* cutting about the arrival of Fleet Street at the Anchor when the Duchess of York briefly took up residence in the nearby village of Chideock while Prince Andrew was at Portland naval base.

Naturally, the menu has plenty of seafood. A popular special is crabmeat on avocado, topped with melted cheese. There are also home-made pies, as well as pizzas, burgers and sandwiches. This is a Palmers house, belonging to the family run brewery at nearby Bridport, so Tally Ho! and Bridport Bitter are available. You can have coffee and a KitKat, if you prefer, at elevenses. There is a children's menu and a family room with a serving hatch leading directly from the kitchen.

The opening hours are 11 am to 2.30 pm, and 7 pm to 11 pm, but in summer (late May to early September) the inn is open all day, 11 am to 11 pm, with food served from noon to 9.30 pm (cream teas between 3 pm and 5.30 pm). On wintertime Sundays the hours are 12 noon to 3 pm and 7 pm to 10.30 pm, with food only available at lunchtime. Summer Sunday opening times are noon to 10.30 pm (although no alcoholic drinks are available 3 pm to 7 pm), and there is food all day.

Telephone: 01297 489215.

*How to get there:* Turn off the A35 at Chideock, between Lyme Regis and Bridport, and continue to Seatown. The inn is at the end of the road, by the sea.

*Parking:* There is a car park opposite the pub.

*Length of the walk:* 2 miles. Map: OS Landranger 193 Taunton and Lyme Regis (inn GR 419918).

*This is a steep, but very rewarding, walk, 626 ft up to the south coast's highest point, known as Golden Cap, where on clear days the view extends west into Devon and east to Portland.*

## The Walk

Go right out of the inn to the coast path signpost by the beach. A path winds up to a flight of steps. At the top, follow the grassy clifftop path, which continues to gain height before the view is lost

*View of the Golden Cap.*

behind bushes. Keep left where the path divides, to reach a stile. The path runs ahead, marked by isolated leaning trees, to climb the east side of the cliff. Near the top there is a handy seat where you should pause to enjoy the fine view behind.

At the side of the seat, stiles lead into a field. Follow the fence on the left up to a kissing gate. Here a waymarked path zig-zags up to the Golden Cap summit. The name comes from the summit's gorse. As well as the trig point, there is a memorial stone to Lord Antrim, one-time chairman of the National Trust which

has protected this remote spot since 1974. Look on the back to see a fossil.

After returning to the kissing gate below, keep forward down to a small gate by a farm gate. Continue through a field to a second gateway to the start of a lane by Langdon Hill Wood. Follow the lane, which has occasional views to the right and runs gently downhill. Some way beyond a gateway another lane joins from the left. At a fork keep right. The narrower left-hand path is the start of Pettycrate Lane leading to Chideock. The walk continues to the right, where the track is known as Combrey Lane.

There are more views as the lane winds downhill to become metalled just before a junction with Sea Hill Lane. Turn right down the main Seatown approach and round a double bend by Seatown Farm House. Note the figure above the window. The road runs directly to the pub.

# 2 Corscombe
## The Fox

The 17th-century inn has a country feel, with its stuffed birds, stuffed fox, mounted hare's head, hunting prints and brasses. The only recent change has been Lisa Comer's wild flower paintings inside the porch. Her work also appears on the walls of the ladies' toilet. The two main bars have open fireplaces and flagstone floors. A more recently added third room, with attractive, rough stone walls, is available for families. In summer the lane outside remains quiet enough for customers to cross over to the seats on the grass next to the stone sheep wash by the stream. This is the best place to view the charming exterior, which has not only a thatched roof but thatched porches. The date over the door is '1709' but local expert opinion claims the inn was here at least a century earlier. Nobody is quite sure when it changed its name from the New Inn to the Fox, except that it was sometime between 1895 and 1899.

Exmoor Ale, Bridport Bitter and Fuller's London Pride are all available at this freehouse. The menu on the blackboard changes slightly each day and, as food is always made to order, this is not a pub for a rushed snack. Indeed, the notice outside proclaims 'no chips or microwave'. The ploughman's lunches include ham, and Shropshire (which means blue cheese). There is often game casserole, fish soup or fish pie. 'Fox's Favourite' is chicken in cream sauce. There are also plenty of puddings, including hot treacle tart with cream.

The opening hours are 12 noon to 2.30 pm and 7 pm to 11 pm, with no afternoon closure on Saturday. On Sunday the hours are 12 noon to 3 pm and 7 pm to 10.30 pm. The inn's proud claim is that it opens every day, *including* Christmas morning.

Telephone: 01935 891330.

*How to get there:* Corscombe lies just north of the A356 Crewkerne to Maiden Newton road. The Fox is at the east end of the village, near Corscombe Court.

*Parking:* There is a small car park at the Fox and some space in the road.

*Length of the walk:* 2½ miles. Map: OS Landranger 194 Dorchester and Weymouth (inn GR 526053).

*Corscombe is just 1½ miles from the county boundary with Somerset, but the quiet lanes still have a Dorset feel. This up-and-down walk is around the scattered village, passing first the 16th-century Corscombe House and the church, which, although rebuilt by the Victorians, still has a medieval tower. After a wood and a viewpoint, the way is downhill to the main street, before crossing more countryside to approach the 13th century, moated Corscombe Court, which once belonged to Sherborne Abbey.*

## The Walk

From the Fox turn left and at once take the right fork. The road crosses a stream and rises. Ignore the first turning to the right and continue uphill to pass the village hall – the former school, which was built in 1872 and closed in 1964. At the next junction (where a signpost confusingly points to 'Corscombe'), still keep ahead, past a Victorian postbox and cottage, and at a junction go left onto a lane which bends round to reach Corscombe House (the former rectory) and church.

Keep past the church where the lane narrows. Soon the way
bends right to give a view down into a valley before bearing left
and descending steeply. At the bottom the wooded lane is still
high above a stream. On reaching a cottage with a white fence,
turn right up to a gate leading into a sloping field.

Go ahead uphill, with a wood to the left. Pass through a line
of trees and still keep uphill. Once over the brow you will see
a gate ahead – it has long been made out of an old notice. From
the gate there is an impressive view down into a long, curving,
dry valley.

Go through the gate and head for a point just right of a small,
lonely tree. Once on the far side you are able to see a fence. Go

through a gate and bear half-left. Head towards a point which is almost at the far corner. Go through a green gate to a lane.

Cross straight over to a larger gate. There is a path waymarked (on the gatepost) ahead but the walk goes half-right across the field. At the fence go through a small gate to continue in the same direction, with a view down into a valley. Go down the side of the steep field to a gate at a field corner.

Beyond the gate, keep forward. The wide way is briefly enclosed. Up on the hill there are chalets. At a junction of paths keep ahead below a wooded bank. The path runs up a steep slope to a viewpoint. Go through the gate to the lane and turn right. This narrow way is Burrow Lane. Soon there is a view over lakes below and the main village street. Follow the winding lane which suddenly widens by some stone houses built as recently as the mid-1980s. Soon you come to Corscombe High Street.

Turn right along the main street. Beyond one of the village notice boards there are Harold's and Jane's cottages, which are even older than the early 18th-century Winton Cottage next door. Beyond a stream the road climbs up to reach the stone Pope's Cottage on the right. The house dates from 1796 and is believed

*Corscombe church and the former rectory.*

to have been associated with the Pope brewing family of Eldridge Pope at Dorchester.

Do not go round the bend with the main road but turn left to pass Pine's Cottage and go up Brickyard Lane. After a short distance, turn right through a gate into a field. The way is ahead downhill at the side of the field to another gate. Cut across a smaller field and go over a stile. Continue straight on near the side of a large field to pass a barn and go through a gateway. Keep ahead to pass in front of Corscombe Court. The archway of the tithe barn can be seen across the courtyard. There may be some black swans from the moat which defends the other three sides of the property. The path meets a road opposite one of village's three postboxes. Turn right for the Fox.

# 3 Powerstock
# The Three Horseshoes

The inn, known locally as simply 'the Shoes', has been in business on the site since the 17th century. The present Edwardian building is the result of a fire in 1906. Inside, the walls are decorated with paintings for sale and a copy of the parish's definitive footpath map. There is a dining room, as this inn is noted for its fine food and dinners, but meals can also be taken in the panelled bar, which has tables and both a meal and bar menu. Outside, the large back garden has a children's swing and climbing frame – and a good view.

This is a Palmers house, so Bridport and Tally Ho! are served. Cider is on draught and a different regional wine is featured each month. Fruit juice is freshly squeezed. The food, listed on two blackboards, always has a strong fish theme, dictated by the local catch – the sea is only 5 miles away. Besides a 'Today's Fish' list there is a 'Today's Meat' which often includes Dorset lamb. Fish soup and filled BLT baguettes are popular with walkers. Favourite puddings here are Dorset trifle

and sticky toffee pudding. The opening hours are 11 am to 3 pm and 6 pm to 11 pm on weekdays, and 12 noon to 3 pm and 7 pm to 10.30 pm on Sundays.
Telephone: 01308 485328.

*How to get there:* Powerstock is to the south of the A356 Crewkerne to Maiden Newton road and is signposted at Kingcombe crossroads.

*Parking:* There is a car park at the side of the inn.

*Length of the walk:* 4 miles. Map: OS Landranger 194 Dorchester and Weymouth (inn GR 517962).

*Powerstock is hidden between the Dorset hills so this walk offers you climbs and sweeping views. The church, which is the village landmark, has Dorset's most elaborate Norman chancel arch and in the churchyard (north-east corner) the tomb of writer and broadcaster Kenneth Allsop. Look for the dole table for loaves to be placed on outside the porch. The route touches on West*

*View of Eggardon Hill from West Milton churchyard.*

*Milton, where the medieval tower of the abandoned church survives, before following a bridleway up onto a viewpoint. The way back is on a gentle metalled lane running downhill.*

### The Walk

Go left out of the pub and walk down to the five-way junction. Turn sharp left down the hill to pass the school. Note its porch and a window which comes from West Milton church, visited later on this walk. At the bottom of the hill and just before the bridge, go right up the side of a house to a gate. Continue ahead, bearing half-right below a high bank. Where this ends join a sheltered path running in the same direction through trees.

19

Beyond a stile and a gate, the way is in the open. Keep forward along the ridged field – there are waymarks on the pole. Down to the left is a stream. There is a gateway, before the path continues ahead, passing close to an oak tree. After a wooden gate near buildings, where the main path soon swings to the left, continue ahead on the narrow, fenced path to cross a bridge. Here at the gate do not bear right with the bridleway but go left up the field towards buildings. The path runs to a stile and into the old churchyard of West Milton. The nave was demolished in 1873, leaving the 15th-century tower standing on the lawn. Looking back to the vanished east end, there is a view of Eggardon Hill.

Walk through the gate and down steps to a lane. Turn right for a few yards, before turning right again up the entrance to Church Farm. A sign says 'Bridleway to Ridgeback Lane'. Just before the farmhouse go through a gate and turn left up a grassy lane. After another gate the way is wooded and later it narrows. Go over the gate at the top and up into the field, where there is a magnificent view on the right.

Keep by the fence on the left. Soon there is a dramatic view left over west Dorset. Down to the right is a valley. On reaching a facing gateway, go through it and up to a second gate leading to a field. Go ahead along the right-hand side of the large field. After 300 yards, where the field boundary has veered gently right into a dent, go down the bank to a gate. The way is now enclosed by hedges as far as Ridgeback Lane.

Turn right along the metalled lane. There is a view half-left of the trig point above Poorton. After passing Springhill Farm, there is a double bend which gives a view of North Poorton church. At a junction go sharp right down a narrow lane.

At the bottom of the hill the lane bends to pass Bottom Farm. Stay in the lane which, although metalled, is at times narrow. After climbing a hill by Poorton Hill Farm there is a double bend with a view north. The lane soon runs downhill into Powerstock. Keep forward past the church for the Three Horseshoes.

# 4 Langton Herring
## The Elm Tree

Langton means 'long farm' and Herring comes from Sir Walter Harang whose family were lords of the manor from the 13th century. The tiny church, although much rebuilt, dates from this period. The Elm Tree is a remarkably good pub. Although most visitors bypass the little village of Langton Herring on their way from Weymouth to the more famous Abbotsbury, there are many who call here just to visit the inn.

The thatched cottage has two bars, with contrasting fireplaces – one being modern and central, and the other an old inglenook, much more in keeping with the beams above. The pub, with its polished brasses and settles, is cosy in winter and has a sheltered garden in summer. This is a Devenish house, with Greenalls, Boddingtons and Whitbread Pompey Royal available, but it is the food which draws many customers. The Elm Tree opens at 10 am on weekdays and serves brunch, with such items as 'Bacon Banjo' (baguette filled with grilled bacon, tomato and melted cheese) which can also be enjoyed at midday. Ploughman's lunches come with a choice of three cheeses, including Dorset Blue

21

Vinny, or roast beef. There are also sandwiches and thick country soup. As many as 20 dishes on the menu carry the vegetarian symbol. Tempting puddings like banana butterscotch fritters are chalked up on a board. From Monday to Saturday the opening hours are 10 am to 2.30 pm and 6.30 pm to 11 pm, with food available until 10 pm. On Sunday the times are 12 noon to 3 pm and 7 pm to 10.30 pm.

Telephone: 01305 871257.

*How to get there:* Langton Herring is off the B3157, between Weymouth and Portesham. The village is signposted at Langton Cross. The Elm Tree is best approached down the turning opposite the phone box.

*Parking:* The Elm Tree has a car park.

*Length of the walk:* 3 miles. Map: OS Landranger 194 Dorchester and Weymouth (inn GR 615824).

*The village is above the Fleet, an 8-mile long lagoon inside Chesil Beach. It was over this lonely water that the Dambusters' Raid was rehearsed with a dummy bouncing bomb in 1943. Today, there are still many swans from the nearby Abbotsbury Swannery, which was started by monks in 1393. Deer sometimes appear here on the coast. The walk goes downhill to find the Dorset Coast Path running along the mainland. The way back is more gentle, taking in Langton Hive Point and a valley path.*

**The Walk**
From the inn's car park entrance go right up Shop Street, passing at once the blacksmith's. Follow the road past a turning and round a bend. At some newer houses the way divides. Turn left in front of Fleet Way Cottage to go up an enclosed track. Soon there is a stile by a gate. Keep ahead along the track and after a short distance there is the first view, half-right, of the Fleet and Chesil Beach. The path begins to descend and veers a little to the left to pass a wood. At the bottom there is another slight bend. Before reaching another gate ahead, leave the path by going right through a gate. A signpost nearby points to the 'Coast Path'.

Cross a footbridge and a stile to follow the coast path along the

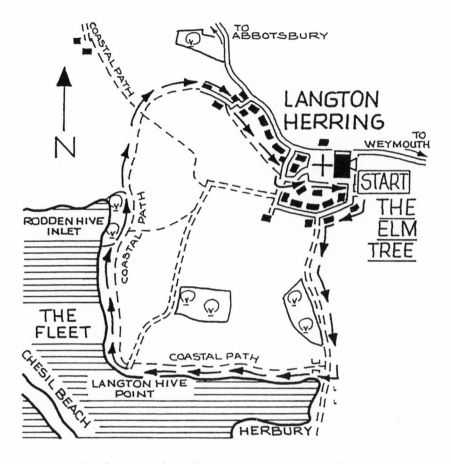

bottom of a field. At first the water is an inlet in the Fleet, with the cultivated land across the water (known as Herbury) being a headland rather than Chesil Beach, which can be seen beyond. This footpath is part of the official national trail and so is well maintained and easy to follow.

At Langton Hive Point stiles take the path across the end of Coastguard Road where there is a slipway. To the south-east can be seen the high ground of Portland sticking out into the English Channel. The path now turns north-west with the coast, giving a view up the Fleet and, soon, into Rodden Hive inlet – hive means 'landing place'.

The path runs inland of a copse. At a large waterside wood

*Fleet and Chesil Beach.*

turn right for a few yards to a signpost. Do not continue ahead up the hill (signposted 'Langton Herring ½') but climb over the stile to walk along the side of the wood. On the way there is a view of the Hardy Monument 3½ miles away on Black Down – this commemorates Admiral Hardy of Trafalgar fame.

Cross a plank footbridge and a couple of stiles to reach a junction of paths. Leave the coast path (which bears left) to go ahead over a stile and down a short, narrow path to another stile. The way now curves gently uphill and soon runs across an open field towards the edge of the village. Go through a gate and up the lane ahead. Before a bend to the left, look out for a stile on the right. Go up the steps and over the stile. After a short distance turn left to follow a stone wall uphill. Over to the left are houses on the Langton Herring road. At the top of the field turn round to see the 14th-century St Catherine's Chapel, built on a hill above Abbotsbury as a navigation guide.

Go over the stile and turn left. At a road go right to pass East Cottage. The lane runs downhill to a junction. Go right uphill to pass between the church and the post office. Next to the church is the Elm Tree and a gate leading into the car park.

# ⑤ Chetnole
## The Chetnole Inn

Chetnole is a small village on the tiny river Wriggle, with the church, inn and post office grouped together at a road junction, in one of the least promoted parts of west Dorset. Locals crowd the small bar, which features music and lots of photographs of partying villagers. The quieter lounge bar has pictures and drawings of Chetnole in past years. There is also a dining room, although many people eat at the lounge tables. In summer the tables outside the front or in the garden at the back are delightful settings for a drink and snack. There is also a skittle alley at the side.

This charming freehouse is renowned for real ales, with at least six pumps on the go in the summer. Local Palmers is always there but, otherwise, there is a changing list, with advance notice given of new arrivals. The inn prides itself on having a 'massive selection of home cooked food' so, besides the ploughman's lunches in many varieties, there are plenty of specials, such as 'Wriggle Valley Duck'. The ham is home-cooked for the ploughman's and

sandwiches, or for serving hot with parsley sauce. There is also a generous pudding list, including treacle sponge, and a children's menu. The times of opening are 11 am to 2.30 pm and 6.30 pm to 11 pm. On Sunday the opening hours are 12 noon to 3 pm and 7 pm to 10.30 pm.
Telephone: 01935 872337.

*How to get there:* Chetnole is off the A37 Yeovil to Dorchester road and just south of Yetminster. The inn is opposite the church. Trains on the Yeovil Pen Mill to Weymouth line stop by request at Chetnole Halt.

*Parking:* There is a car park at the side of the inn and parking is allowed in the road by the churchyard wall.

*Length of the walk:* 3 miles. Map: OS Landranger 194 Dorchester and Weymouth (inn GR 602083).

*On this walk each church is smaller than the last. The first, in Chetnole, has a 13th-century nave and an only slightly later tower. The second, in a charming setting alongside the Melbury Bubb manor house, is noted for its mysterious upside-down font. After climbing to a hill viewpoint, spectacularly marked by strip lynchets, the way is down to England's smallest church, found in the quiet corner of a field.*

## The Walk
Turn right to the road junction and go left to pass the church gateway. Continue down the village's main street. On the left there is Mill Lane, before reaching the main junction and a signpost. Walk just past the sharp right turning and go right to a gateway.
   Pass through the gate and along the side of a garden to another gate, which leads into a field. Go ahead along the side of the field. At the next corner go through the gate and bear half-right towards the middle of the far side. In the hedge there are two stiles, linked by a short footbridge. On the far side is a narrow end of a field. Bear half-right to soon follow a hedge on the left. Keep by this hedge, which curves round to the other narrow end of the field. Here go through the gate and over the railway bridge. Ahead are

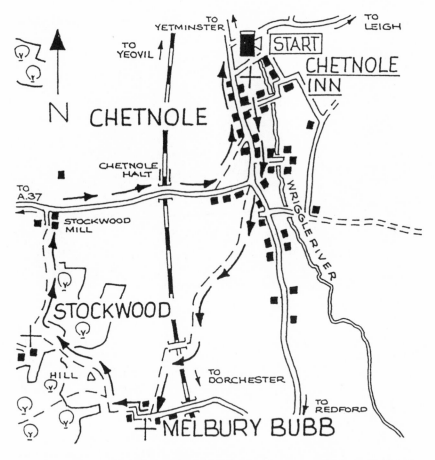

two gateways. Go through the left-hand one and bear half-left towards the church tower. At the far corner go through a gate and turn right. Go beyond the turning and past the postbox to the end of the road. To the left a grass path leads up to the churchyard gates of Melbury Bubb church.

The tower was built in 1474, although most of the rest of the church was rebuilt in 1854, retaining some original stained glass. Lighting is by paraffin lamp. Surviving from Norman times is the unusual font, where carved animals are upside down. It is probably the base of an Anglo-Saxon cross, hollowed out for new use. Turn the picture on the church leaflet upside down to see the carved stag.

*Stockwood church, England's smallest church.*

The walk continues opposite the churchyard gate. Ignore the private sign for cars and go up the farm track, which bends to follow the wall of the 17th-century manor house. Go directly ahead and through a gate. Walk past a barn (left) and through another gate into a large, sloping field. Ahead is a small building. Walk uphill to keep the building on the right. Once past the building, turn right to walk up to a gateway. Beyond the gate keep by the fence on the right, where there is a view. After a short distance bear left over to the nearby trig point.

Here there is a good view north. Below can be seen a lane. Turn north-west in this direction and very shortly a gate can be seen below. Go down the steep, ridged hill to the gate on the edge of the wood and cross the stile at the side. Follow the woodland track which later curves round to the left to a gate leading into a field. Bear half-right across the field towards Stockwood church. A track runs into the next field where there is a bridge leading to the churchyard. The gate may be untied by those visiting the church.

This is the smallest church in England and the only one dedicated to St Edwold, brother of St Edmund. The building, which once had its own priest, dates from the early 15th century, with the bell turret added in 1636.

On leaving the church gate (which should be tied up), continue ahead across the field to go through a farm gate opposite. At once, turn right over the field to a stile under the oak tree. Keep ahead, with the wood to the right. Soon, when the trees end, there is a view of Stockwood Mill.

Keep forward to a stile between the two oaks ahead. Beware the big step down into the road. Turn right along the road – walking on the right-hand side. On crossing the railway, there is a view left of Yetminster church tower. Continue downhill to the 30 mph signs. On the left, behind the 'Chetnole' sign, go left over a stile in the hedge.

Keep ahead along the side of a field and into a large field. Continue forward by the side of the field, with a view of the village ahead. At the far end, go through a wooden gate tucked in the corner. Go right along a short lane to a junction by Foys Lodge. Turn left up the main street to the church and the Chetnole Inn.

# 6 Cerne Abbas
## The New Inn

Cerne Abbas is a former small town which grew up around the Benedictine monastery, but later flourished as a centre of brewing – there were once 13 inns here. The New Inn is very old and claims to have been the abbey guest house as early as Henry IV's reign, when the existing guest house at the end of Abbey Street was still the abbot's residence. The inn, standing on the old, wide, through road, survived the closure of the monastery in 1539 to become an important coaching inn. The courtyard's pump, dated 1774, and mounting block are from this period. However, the stone roof and mullioned windows recall the pre-Reformation days. The area in front of the fireplace was used as a court as recently as 1860, with the present ladies' toilet being the prisoners' cell. Until the First World War, tenants on the Pitt-Rivers estate came here to pay their rents, with the incentive of receiving a threepenny beer token.

As this is an Eldridge Pope house, Hardy and Royal Oak ales are available. The menu is chalked up on a board by the door.

There are usually Brie, pâté and Stilton ploughman's lunches, soup and omelettes. A speciality is toad-in-the-hole and there is always at least one vegetarian main course available. Children are welcome in the bar eating area and in summer there are tables on the lawn of the large garden at the back. The New Inn is open from 12 noon to 3 pm and 6 pm to 11.30 pm. On Sunday the hours are 12 noon to 3 pm and 7 pm to 10.30 pm.

Telephone: 01300 341274.

*How to get there:* Cerne Abbas lies on the A352, between Dorchester and Sherborne. The New Inn is in Long Street, east off the main road.

*Parking:* There is plenty of parking space in the wide street outside.

*Length of the walk:* 2½ miles (a short-cut, leaving out Giant Hill, is possible). Map: OS Landranger 194 Dorchester and Weymouth (inn GR 664011).

*This walk visits the abbey remains and takes in a good view of the famous giant, before climbing up to pass the giant's toes and the prehistoric earthworks on Giant Hill. The 180 ft high figure cut in chalk (maybe around AD 180 by the Romans) is thought to be a pagan fertility symbol. As late as the early 19th century, women still slept by the giant on the hill, although in monastic times women had prayed for childbirth at St Catherine's Shrine at the abbey. Legend has it that this is the outline of a real giant who lay down on the hill and was killed by shepherds.*

**The Walk**
Walk up Duck Street which is opposite the New Inn. Go beyond the last house to go right down a lane, signposted 'pottery'. Soon there is a view half-left, between two trees, of the giant on the hill. There is another good view of the giant just beyond this turning.

Do not cross Kettle Bridge but turn right along the path which follows the Cerne river. Cross the footbridge and go along a passage to Abbey Street. Those who do not wish to climb up Giant's Hill can turn right to the church and right again to return to the New Inn.

The walk continues to the left, past the town pond. Bear right to the gateways and go through the right-hand one into the cemetery. Follow the path half-left to go through the gate on the far side. Continue half-right (but not right) to the trees ahead. The grass here covers the site of the abbey church. The other guest house, with its oriel window, can be seen over to the left. Go past a cattle trough and up to a stile.

Once over the stile go right up the wooded slope and at a junction go left. Soon the path is in the open and ahead there is a National Trust sign. Keep to the left of the sign to follow a fence along the bottom of the giant. Towards the end of the fence

*Path through cemetery to Giant's Hill.*

it is possible to see the feet – the rest of the body is over the brow of the hill.

The path runs beyond the fence and along the ridged side of the open hillside. Later, the way becomes a clear, wide, grass path running up the hill to pass through bushes before reaching the top of the hill. Here there is a magnificent view to the left. Below can be seen Up Cerne manor house and church. Ahead there is a fence at an angle. Go over the stile and head towards the barn at the side of the wood. On approaching the barn there can be seen a gateway and stile. Do not go over the stile to the barn but turn right along the side of the field, keeping by the fence on the left. To the right can be seen the Hardy Monument near the coast (see Walk 4).

At the corner of the field go through the smaller gate and turn right to follow a fence. After 200 yards the fence has a gate and begins to bear right by some bushes. Here leave the fence to bear half-left, keeping the bushes on the right. As the ground begins to drop a path is seen running ahead, downhill. For a time it is like a grassy causeway before becoming slightly stony and narrower. Below can be seen a long hedge, marking the line of Yelcome Drove. The path is less steep as it runs through trees near the bottom.

When the way is again in the open and begins to curve down to the left, go over a set-back stile up on the right. Keep in the direction of the church tower, following the raised ground which is part of the monastery site. On coming up against a ditch, bear round to the right and then turn left to walk down to the cemetery. Go up Abbey Street to pass the church and turn right to the New Inn.

# Osmington
## The Sunray

Osmington's several thatched cottages include the post office and some 1990s building. The church dates from the 13th century and has an early Tudor tower. The village was artist John Constable's honeymoon destination in 1816 when he stayed at the Old Vicarage. His *Weymouth Bay* in the National Gallery remains half finished, but his friendship with the vicar led to the commissions for the famous Salisbury Cathedral series. The Sunray, on the main Weymouth—Wool coast road, consists of two older buildings joined together by a modern link. The new structure's interior is 'older' than expected, with beams in the low ceiling and plenty of old cups and toby jugs on the shelves. The pub has long been well known for welcoming children and an impressive climbing frame dominates the garden. Inside, there is a pirate theme children's menu featuring six chip meals, including fish boats and vegetable fingers. The 'desserters' have such names as 'Ah-ha Me Smarties' – ice–cream, wafer, cream, and Smarties. The adult menu is also adventurous, with mushroom and ale pie and sesame chicken fillets. Sandwich fillings are honey roast ham and turkey with cranberry. Desserts include sticky toffee pudding and 'Ho Ho Ice Cream Sundae', which is also found on the children's menu. There are always three real ales, for example, Thomas Hardy Country and Flowers, as well as, of course, plenty of soft drinks. The Sunray is open from 11 am to 3 pm and 5.30 pm to 11 pm, but in summer the hours are 11 am to 11 pm. The Sunday opening hours are 12 noon to 4 pm and 6 pm to 10.30 pm.

Telephone: 01305 832148.

*How to get there:* Osmington lies on the A353, between Weymouth and Warmwell. The inn is on a corner of the main road, opposite the thatched bus shelter.

*Parking:* The Sunray has a large car park.

*Length of the walk:* 3¹/₂ miles. Map: OS Landranger 194 Dorchester and Weymouth (inn GR 725828).

*The White Horse on the hill behind Osmington, completed in 1808, was cut by army engineers. The figure on horseback is George III, who spent his holidays in nearby Weymouth. This route goes up to the viewpoint above the 180 ft figure and along a ridge, with panoramic views of Weymouth and Portland.*

## The Walk
Turn left out of the Sunray and walk down the village street. At the end turn left again and at the next corner, by the post office, go right. At once the Beehive is on the left and soon there are several houses offering bed and breakfast. This accommodation can be described as being 'on the Dorset Coast Path' as this lane is part of the inland alternative for those wishing to avoid Weymouth.

At a junction there is the village pump. Keep forward and just beyond Hall's Farm entrance there is a view half-left up to the White Horse. Do not go into the field, but continue up the lane, which becomes rough. After a stile by a gate the track veers to the left to begin ascending the hill. On the way, Weymouth Bay comes into view.

Continue all the way to the top, where there is a signpost and

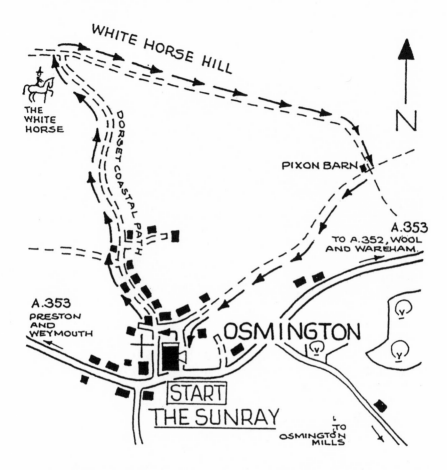

a view of Weymouth and the coast, including Portland. The coast path turns left through the gate, whilst the walk continues to the right in the direction of Poxwell.

Soon the bridleway becomes fenced and there are several gates along the way. As the path bends on the ridge, the view south is replaced with a view north of the forest between the Frome and Piddle valleys. Later the way opens out into a wide drove and bears round to the right to a gate. Ahead is a view of White Nothe cliff, which has long been known as 'White Nose', after the suggestion that it resembled the famous Duke of Wellington's nose.

The path now runs gently downhill, through another gate, and

*View above the village of Osmington.*

along the side of a sloping field. An indentation in the middle of the field is the remains of a Romano-British grain pit. There is also a view east down to Poxwell Manor House. Poxwell's ancient well can be found on the south side of the field.

Pass Pixon Barn, over the wall to the right, and go through the gate ahead. Turn right up to another gate and go through the left-hand of the two ahead. The path gives a view left, down into the Osmington Mills valley on the coast and ahead to Portland. Later, the White Horse comes into view over to the right. Stay on this path, which in places is clearly defined, as it drops down through gateways to pass through trees near the bottom. At Osmington go left up the village street for the Sunray.

# 8 Sturminster Newton
## The White Hart

Sturminster Newton is a small town, with the river Stour on two sides, and very quiet, except on Monday – which is market day. The locals just call it 'Stur' but it was known as Sturminster Newton Castle (after the earthwork to the south) so Thomas Hardy, who lived here, called it 'Stourcastle' in *Tess of the d'Urbervilles*. This was also the childhood home of Dorset poet William Barnes (1801–1866), who used to sit on the cross opposite the White Hart. The 18th-century thatched coaching inn has the date '1708' on the front wall, confirming that it survived the 1729 fire which damaged the town centre. There were several bars but now the ground floor is just a single one. It still feels cosy, with a low, beamed ceiling and comfortable window seats. There is a notice board for local events as well as leaflets for the tourists who drive down from Somerset. This is a Hall & Woodhouse inn, so there is Badger beer available from the nearby Blandford brewery. The blackboard at each end of the long bar always features soup and ploughman's lunches. You are

39

also likely to find steak and kidney pie, cottage pie and a couple of fish dishes. The Cumberland sausage comes rolled up in a bap with salad. Children's portions can be ordered. The sweets are traditional, such as treacle pudding and spotted dick. The times of opening are from 10.30 am to 3 pm and 6.30 pm to 11 pm, but there is no afternoon closure on Friday and Saturday. The Sunday opening hours are 12 noon to 3 pm and 7 pm to 10.30 pm. Food is available from 12 noon to 2 pm and 7 pm to 9 pm.

Telephone: 01258 472593.

*How to get there:* Sturminster Newton is off the A357, between Blandford Forum and Sherborne. The small town is signposted at Newton.

*Parking:* There is a car park under the arch at the White Hart. Alternatively, there is a public car park opposite the cattle market.

*Length of the walk:* 3 miles (or less, if you leave out the walk to Fiddleford Mill). Map: OS Landranger 194 Dorchester and Weymouth (inn GR 786141).

*The walk circles the tiny town, passing two mills and a medieval manor house that has a spectacular interior open to the public.*

**The Walk**
Turn right out of the White Hart and at once go right, down Rickett's Lane, to follow the path along the side of the recreation ground. At the end there is, on the right, Riverside, where Thomas Hardy lived between 1876 and 1878 when writing *The Return of the Native*.

At the river Stour turn left to go behind the shelter and through the kissing gate. Follow the tread in the grass, which runs a quarter-left with the river over to the right. Keep forward through a kissing gate and over two bridges to Sturminster Newton Mill. This is a late 17th-century building, but the Domesday Book records a mill here in 1086. The working mill is often open to visitors. Turn left round the back of it to walk up to the main road.

Go left to follow the pavement by the river. This is the edge of

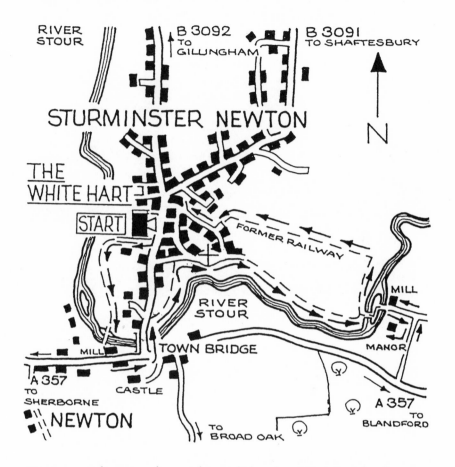

Newton and across the road a path by the old chapel leads up to the castle – a ruined manor house standing within an Iron Age earthworks. The walk continues to the left over the 15th-century Town Bridge, built by the Abbot of Glastonbury Abbey, which owned the house in the Iron Age fort. Look at the notice on the bridge warning of deportation for vandals.

Follow the causeway road ahead towards Bridge Street, to go right through the kissing gate by an iron gate. The curving path, known as the Coach Road, was the driveway to the vicarage – now Southbank. On approaching another drive gate, turn left to go through a kissing gate. Continue up the steep, enclosed path to a junction with a lane.

*The Town Bridge, Sturminster Newton.*

Turn right to see the church ahead. This is Stur's minster, from which the town takes its name. The nave and aisles date from 1486, when the Abbot of Glastonbury, who was lord of the manor, directed the work. The carved lectern commemorates William Barnes. In the window on the south side St Elizabeth and the Child are portraits of a mother and son who lived at Vine House – the mother died of flu when the child was still a baby.

Keep the church to the left to walk through the churchyard. Go down a few steps and past a cottage called Tanyard (dating from the 13th century). The lane bends to the left.

*To shorten the walk*, continue ahead along Penny Street – see last paragraph.

*For the main walk*, turn right up a path next to Ham Gate and continue along the hedged track to a stile by a gate. From the gateway bear half-right across the field. The river is over to the right and ahead in the distance can be seen Hambledon Hill. Head for the oak trees, below which the hedge double bends. Here there is a gate and a stile. Once in the next field go left, following the hedge on the left. After a gap leading to the next field, bear slightly to the right on a path over the meadow. At the far end go over a footbridge on the left and bear right to a bridge crossing the river.

The bridge leads to Fiddleford Mill, which has the date 1566 in the wall, and the Manor House, dating from the 14th century. To visit the house, in the care of English Heritage and open daily (admission free), go ahead and turn right, going right again through the grass car park. Upstairs there is a fragment of wall painting. In the same room look up the chimney – wide enough for Father Christmas to get down – to see the sky.

Only cross the bridge to see the mill or visit the house. The walk continues from the west side of the bridge. Turn left to follow the river bank to the site of the railway bridge. Go over the stile and at once bear left to go up steps to reach the top of the low railway embankment. This was the Somerset & Dorset line until 1966 and since then trees, bushes and wildflowers have taken over. Follow the line, which runs directly to the town.

After crossing a bridge, continue for a short distance before turning left down steps to a stile. Go ahead along the side of the field and climb over a stile on the right. A path known as Gott's Corner runs to a junction. Turn right up Penny Lane to pass Bathurst.

Further up on the right is the 17th-century, stone Vine House, where William Barnes worked briefly when it was a solicitor's. After passing Sturminster Printers, go left into Church Street and right for the cross opposite the White Hart.

# 9 Spetisbury
# The Drax Arms

'11 miles Poole 3 miles Blandford' says the milestone outside the cottage next to the Drax Arms. On the far side of the inn is the thatched Marigold Cottage, where a board announces 'This cottage has stood through the following reigns', above a list starting with Henry VIII. The Drax Arms was also thatched until a fire forced a complete rebuild in 1926. The inside of the pub is very homely, with pictures of Edward VII and Queen Alexandra on the wall and bookshelves containing dictionaries, Halsbury law books and a Solzhenitsyn title. A notice on the door says 'Please do not allow the cat out of the door'.

The inn belonged to the Drax family of Charborough Park, 2 miles to the south, who also owned another Drax Arms at Bere Regis. Hall & Woodhouse now own both and Spetisbury's Drax Arms offers Badger ales. A special attraction is the Isis water which comes from a source 1/2 mile away at Charlton Barrow.

The food includes home-made steak and kidney pie, as well as ham and Stilton ploughman's lunches. Specials on the boards above the bar can include French onion soup, liver and sausage casserole, home-cooked gammon with leek sauce and the 'Drax Fry', featuring corned beef fritters. The Drax Arms is open from 11 am to 3 pm and 6 pm to 11 pm. On Sunday the opening hours are 12 noon to 3 pm and 7 pm to 10.30 pm. The garden at the side has a swing and a see-saw.

Telephone: 01258 452658.

*How to get there:* Spetisbury is on the A350, just south-east of Blandford Forum. The Drax Arms is at the west end of the village.

*Parking:* The inn has a car park at the back.

*Length of the walk:* 2¼ miles. Map: OS Landranger 195 Bournemouth and Purbeck (inn GR 911027).

*Spetisbury is in the Stour valley and this walk goes across the braids of the river, visiting mills on both sides before returning along the former Somerset & Dorset railway line, which avoids a busy main road. Whilst water is bottled on the south side of the valley, wine and cider are produced in the vineyards and orchards of Keynston Mill Fruit Farm on the north side, where visitors are welcome all year. On the way to the meadows the route passes a church with an unusual tomb.*

**The Walk**
Turn right out of the Drax Arms to pass Marigold Cottage. Cross the road and walk on the left-hand side. The pavement gives a good view of Cedar Court and becomes fenced on reaching the church. There is a view down to the porch and the pyramid tomb of a former vicar, Thomas Rackett. The church's tower is medieval and its pulpit has an hour-glass stand.

Continue past the school to a crossroads. Turn right up the entrance to Clapcott's Farm. A clear stream flows to the right. The path swings away from the stream to pass the farm, on the left. Keep to the left of a double garage to pass a cottage and walk on to cross a long, narrow footbridge which spans the stream and part of a garden.

At buildings go right over a bridge at Mill House and left with the path, to pass over more water by the mill pond. The way is

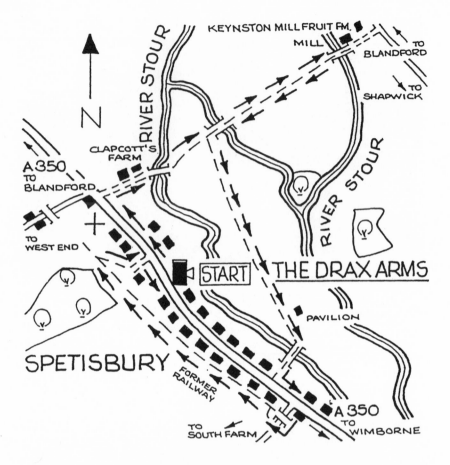

through trees to a gate leading to meadows. Keep ahead towards a line of trees to cross a footbridge over the river Stour, which flows from Stourhead in Wiltshire to Christchurch Harbour. Still keep forward – there is a small footbridge over a flood channel. On the far side, go ahead over a footbridge spanning another Stour channel.

Walk past Keynston Mill and up to Keynston Mill Fruit Farm. The shop and Millwheel restaurant are part of the 6-acre vineyard, where visitors are welcome to wander.

Return down to the mill and cross the river. (An alternative path nearby requires fording the river.) Continue back over the grass to cross the second course of the Stour. At once, turn left

46

*The Rackett tomb in the churchyard at Spetisbury.*

and soon there is a stile to cross. Now bear half-right towards the hill in the distance. At first the path may not be clear on the ground although it runs down the centre of this 'island'. By the third field the path has moved nearer the third braid of the river, on the right. Village back gardens are in sight as the path passes behind the cricket pavilion. Cross the footbridge by the ford and go up to the main road. If you want to return to the Drax Arms at this point, go right.

The walk continues to the left. After a short distance, turn right up a lane marked 'Bridleway to South Farm'. Go under the railway bridge and at once turn left up some steps. At the top the path touches the bottom of the old Spetisbury Halt platform. Trains ceased stopping in 1952 and the last train ran through here 14 years later. Turn left along the former line. At first the way is narrow and soon there is a view over the village to the meadows behind. Later the path widens and runs through a cutting. Beyond a gateway, beneath a bridge, the way is deep and wooded. On emerging from the cutting at once turn right over a stile.

Bear right up the field to a gate and stile on the left. Walk down the stony lane to the main road. Opposite is Marigold Cottage, which is next to the Drax Arms.

# 10 Tolpuddle
## The Martyrs Inn

Tolpuddle is famous for the men who were arrested and deported for starting a farm labourers' 'trade union', although all six were unaware that they had broken the law. Indeed, they eventually received a free pardon. The present inn dates from 1929 but the original building, described in 1848 as a 'beer retailer' and situated nearer the road, was probably standing in 1834 when the Tolpuddle Martyrs were meeting in the village. Since the prosecution against the farm workers was brought by the Crown, it is maybe appropriate that for years the inn was called the Crown. Hall & Woodhouse changed the name in 1979 and now the walls are covered with fascinating material, rivalling in some respects the little museum at the TUC cottages. A print shows Martyr George Loveless in chains on top of a coach in snowy Salisbury on his way to Australia. Photographs include one of TUC General Secretary Vic Feather pulling a pint here at the renaming. Most union leaders and leading Labour MPs have visited the pub during one of the annual memorial rallies, when a procession of banners passes the door. For those wanting all the historical details, there are local history books to read over a drink.

Blandford ales are available, but exclusive to the inn is the strong Martyrs Ale, which is popular not just as a souvenir but also among the villagers. The ploughman's lunches have Dorset Blue Vinny cheese and there is home-made local game or rabbit pie. The blue cheese is also served with steak. At least three home-made vegetarian meals appear on the menu, including nut and mushroom stroganoff, and there are two vegan dishes. Children are welcome in the eating area. The inn is open from 11 am to 2.30 pm and 6 pm to 11 pm. On Sunday the hours are 12 noon to 3 pm and 7 pm to 10.30 pm. In summer there is no afternoon closure and cream teas are available.

Telephone: 01305 848249.

*How to get there:* Tolpuddle is on the A35, between Dorchester and Bere Regis.

*Parking:* There is a car park at the Martyrs Inn.

*Length of the walk:* 4 miles. Map: OS Landranger 194 Dorchester and Weymouth (inn GR 794944).

*The walk passes the historic tree where the fateful outdoor discussions were held, the church where the one Martyr who returned home is buried, and the TUC memorial cottages and museum. The route then explores the high fields behind the village, where farm work continues.*

## The Walk
Turn right out of the inn and walk along the main road. To the left is Forge Cottage. Stay on the road to pass the green, where there is the Martyrs' Tree and a National Trust information board below the thatched shelter. At the top of the slight hill there is the 13th century church. The grave of Tolpuddle Martyr James Hammett is on the west side of the churchyard. Shortly before reaching the TUC cottages, turn right up a track marked 'bridleway to Dewlish'. (In the centre of the line of cottages there is a museum which may be visited.)

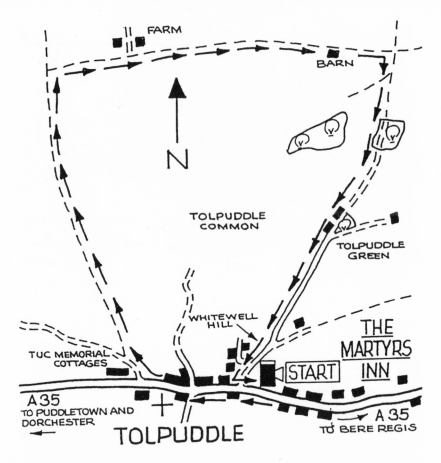

The bridleway bends near the back of the cottages, before heading into a narrow tree-filled hollow. The path climbs gently for 300 yards up to a gate at a field. Continue half-left across the field to a gateway on the far side. The path now follows a hedge (right) as the way rises. There is a splendid view west over a patchwork of fields between Puddletown and Dewlish and south to the coastal hills. Soon after another gate, the path begins a gentle descent and by some trees leaves the field to continue downhill, more steeply, in a wooded hollow.

Soon after reaching the bottom of the hill, look for a turning to the right (there is a small waymark) and follow the hedge along the bottom of the valley. After crossing a track by some farm

*The Martyrs' Tree and its successor.*

buildings, there is a tumulus just apparent over to the right. Stay by the edge of the field and at the far end go over a stile. The way is enclosed to a small gate. Still continue ahead along the valley bottom to pass a barn (right) and go over a stile. Ahead is a high wooded hill fort known as Weatherby Castle. At the far end of the field go through the gate. There is a line of beeches on the left. After a few yards bear round to the right to walk uphill.

On the way up the hill do not turn off to the right with the track marks, but keep on up to the top right-hand corner of the sloping field. Go over a gate and up a wooded track. At the far end there is another gate and a fine view south-east over Wareham Forest to the Purbeck Hills.

Keep by the hedge, which is on the right. In the next field the hedge is to the left but afterwards the way becomes an enclosed lane, running down through a farm at Tolpuddle Common. From here the road is metalled as it goes uphill and then steeply down Whitehill Lane into Tolpuddle. Turn left for the Martyrs Inn.

# 11 West Lulworth
## The Castle Inn

This thatched inn, dating from the early 17th century, used to be called the Jolly Sailor but now takes its name from the nearby Lulworth Castle, depicted on the inn sign. The castle, 2 miles away at East Lulworth, dates from 1608 and was the seat of the Weld family, who own much of the countryside here. Sir Robert Peel and the exiled Charles X of France both lived there for a time. The castle has only recently been re-opened to the public following a fire in 1929, which destroyed the interior and kept the landmark closed for 65 years. In the same year the pub was also hit by a very serious fire, although today one would not suspect it. The restoration is convincing and some claim that the pub even retains its ghost. One landlord is said to have seen a blue light dancing over the chest containing his late wife's belongings. Only when he at last complied with the will and passed the box to his daughter did the mysterious light cease to appear.

The pub interior consists of two bars – a flagstoned public bar, with lots of alcoves for sitting in, and a lounge bar. At the back there is a very well cared for terraced garden and in summer visitors sit outside at both the back and front of the building. In the front there are giant chess and draughts sets, with the boards painted on the ground. This is a Devenish house, with Wessex Bitter, JD Dry Hop, Newquay Steam Bitter, Flowers Original, Marston's Pedigree and several ciders available. The menu is chalked up on a blackboard in the main bar. Ploughman's lunches include ham, Brie, turkey and even fish versions. The choice of casseroles extends to venison, bacon, pigeon and game. There are home-made pies and, sometimes, jugged hare. There are always fish and vegetarian dishes. Children are welcome in the bar eating area and there is a children's menu. The Castle's opening hours are 11 am to 2.30 pm and 7 pm to 11 pm, with food available from noon to 2 pm and 7 pm to 10.30 pm. On Sunday the opening times are 12 noon to 3 pm and 7 pm to 10.30 pm.

Telephone: 01929 941311.

*How to get there:* West Lulworth is on the B3070 Wareham to Lulworth Cove road. The Castle Inn is on the right near the beginning of the village.

*Parking:* The inn has a car park opposite and there is also a large car park near Lulworth Cove at the south end of the village.

*Length of the walk:* 2½ miles. Map: OS Landranger 194 Dorchester and Weymouth (inn GR 826807).

*This walk sets off along the fascinating main street, then climbs the hill behind the Castle. It involves little road walking and rewards you with fine views of the coast and countryside. The route is entirely on the Weld Estate, which has opened up numerous paths and bridleways as permissive paths for public enjoyment.*

**The Walk**
From the Castle Inn forecourt turn right down the main street to pass the old churchyard. The parish church stood here from pre-Norman times until the Victorians built a new one nearby. By the thatched bus shelter look up to see a postbox, preserved high up in a wall.

Keep to the right of the war memorial to go up West Road.

*Churchfield House.*

On the right is Churchfield House, which was the Red Lion when George III used to stop off here for lunch on the way to Weymouth. Later it was a rented holiday home for Sidney Webb, who drafted the Labour Party's Clause IV, and poet Rupert Brooke.

Walk up the road to find a flight of steps on the right. Go up into the trees and straight ahead at a junction. Go over a stile and continue up a field. The way rises gently, with a fine view behind down into Lulworth, with Hambury Tout hill just blocking a view of Portland. Continue up the hill and soon the view improves to the west whilst to the south-east there is a view down across Arish Mell into Worbarrow Bay. There may be the sound of firing from the army ranges or the noise of a rescue helicopter but neither disturbs the deer which wander up here. At the cross-track by the television mast near the top, there is a fine view (on a clear day) of St Aldhelm's Head, with its chapel, sticking out into the sea to the east.

Go over the cross-track and into another field. Over to the right is a trig point and to the left there is a fine view of the patchwork of fields. Keep ahead through a gap and over a stile into another field. The path begins to descend. At the far end of

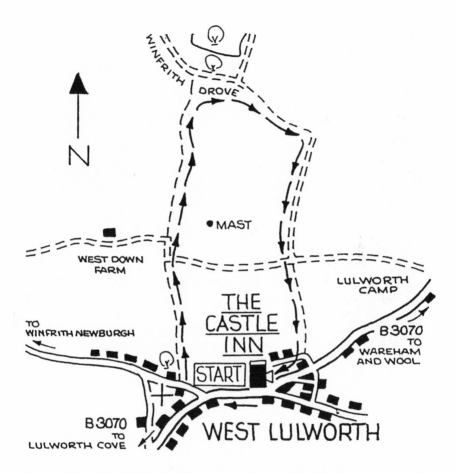

the mainly blackthorn hedge, go over a stile and on a few yards into a green lane. This narrow path is Winfrith Drove, which was used for moving cattle at least as early as Tudor times. Turn right along the woodland path. Soon there is a view north to the forest plantations beyond Wool. Grouse and pheasants are often found along this path, which ends at a stile. Here, keep forward with the field boundary (right) to go down and up to a gate on the right.

Turn right through this gate to follow a track southwards. At a T-junction go ahead down a footpath by a hedge. Keep downhill through three fields to a wooden stile by an end house at the back of the village. Keep forward to a crossroads by Farm Lane and turn right down the main road pavement to the Castle Inn.

# 12 Worth Matravers
## The Square & Compass

This is a 17th-century farmhouse which became a pub in 1752. It was first the Sloop but since the 1830s the name has been the Square & Compass, after the tools used by the local stonemasons. Indeed, the pub is the venue for an annual sculpture festival involving leading Dorset masons. The whitewashed stone building still looks like a farmhouse, especially with the geese and chickens wandering about outside. This is mainly because it has been run by the Newman family since 1907 and the present generation secured its future by buying the historic building from Whitbread. The first Charles Newman entertained many famous people, among them artist Augustus John. The crowded walls in the two front rooms include a cartoon by Leon Heron of Charles chasing butterflies and a drawing by cartoonist Low of Augustus John. There is also a painting of John's local friend, Billy 'Winspit'.

This pub is as John would have known it so the menu is not extensive, but there are always pasties. Nuts and crisps are the most modern addition to the menu. The beers are Ringwood,

Badger Best, Strong Country and Whitbread Pompey Royal. The times of opening are 11 am to 3 pm and 6 pm to 11 pm, and on summer Saturdays there is no afternoon closure. On Sunday the hours are 12 noon to 3 pm and 7 pm to 10.30 pm.

Telephone: 01929 439229.

*How to get there:* Worth Matravers lies off the B3069 Swanage to Kingston road. The Square & Compass is at the junction of the northern and eastern (Swanage) entrances to the village.

*Parking:* The Square & Compass does not have a car park but there is a National Trust car park just a few yards up the northern road beside the pub.

*Length of the walk:* 4 miles. Map: OS Landranger 195 Bournemouth and Purbeck (inn GR 974776).

*From the pub there is a view of the chapel high up on St Aldhelm's Head, which is reached on this walk by way of the pretty village pond and the Norman parish church. The path out to the headland also passes a working quarry which has provided for many famous buildings. After a clifftop walk, where numerous sea birds swoop, there is a valley path, where the warbler or flycatcher may be seen.*

*The clifftop path is very close to the edge. Parents who prefer not to take children on the round route will still find the walk out to the chapel and back most rewarding.*

## The Walk

From the pub front door go ahead down the slope and turn right to reach the village green and pond. Keep ahead past the post office and tea shop. Note the gateposts, which have stone figures of St Nicholas by local mason Valentine Quinn. At the top of the hill there is St Nicholas' church. Go inside and look above the door to find the mirror from the *Halsewell*, which foundered off the coast one night in 1786. Five drowned girls are said to have looked in the mirror to brush their hair before going to bed on the fatal night.

Continue round the double bend and follow the road as far as Weston Farm. Here, keep to the left of Old Harry Cottage up the farm track. After a few yards go right over a stile. Beyond a second stile the way is alongside a field – watch out for half buried sections of an old fence which can cause walkers to trip. Towards the end of the path there is a view half-right of Renscombe Farm, which once belonged to the Benedictine monks at Cerne Abbas.

On meeting a track at a stile, turn left. This track runs directly to St Aldhelm's Head and on the way passes the small St Aldhelm's Head Quarry, first worked in the 12th century. This century some stone from here has been used for Salisbury Cathedral's high altar and for relaying the floor of the Whitehall Banqueting House.

After the quarry the path turns south-west to reach the lonely chapel. This is always open although services are now only held occasionally, such as at dawn on Easter morning when the dark building is lit by over 100 candles. The terrace of cottages was built for the coastguard service, which once had a permanent lookout here. It was near here from 1940 to 1942 that the RAF carried out crucial radar research.

Turn left at the clifftop lookout building to walk eastwards. In the distance can be seen the lighthouse at Durlston. The path is

*St Aldhelm's chapel.*

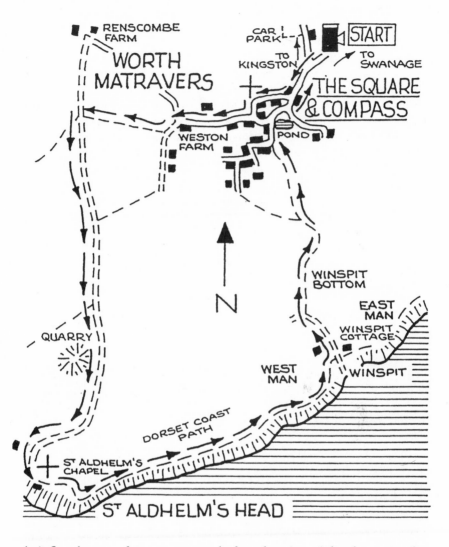

briefly above a former quarry before bearing right down to the
edge of the cliff. Here, the way is on the cliff edge and just outside
a field fence. Soon the path does a double bend, giving a view back
to the base of St Aldhelm's Head. The narrow path, which should
not be left, is fringed with sea cabbage and purple thistle.

After ½ mile the path turns sharply inland to rise up round
the former Winspit quarry and descend into the valley. Turn left

inland along the track up Winspit Bottom, passing the gateway on the right to the 17th-century quarryman's Winspit Cottage, where Augustus John stayed. His host was Billy 'Winspit', who lived here without electricity and with only a well for water. This path was their route up to the Square & Compass.

Go over the stile by the gate ahead. The track bends up the valley but, just before the way becomes metalled, turn right where a sign says 'Worth ½'. The enclosed path leads to a stile and then the way is slightly left uphill. On the way there is a view across to the strip lynchets, indicating a medieval field system on the far hillside.

After a stile a narrow path leads to stiles at a lane. Go ahead and right to reach the pond at Worth Matravers. Follow the road uphill and go right at a T-junction for the Square & Compass.

# 13 Wareham
## The King's Arms

The small town of Wareham lies on high ground between the rivers Piddle and Frome – the latter being the northern boundary of the 'Isle of Purbeck'. Ever since a fire swept the centre in 1762, destroying 876 houses, no new thatched buildings have been allowed. Although it is in the main street, however, the King's Arms does have a thatched roof, because it escaped the spreading flames. Built around 1500, it remains unmodernised, with homely tables and chairs and an inglenook fireplace. Framed photographs show the area in years gone by.

The beers are Whitbread and Murphy's Irish Stout and the food is simple, in keeping with the house. Cheese and ham sandwiches and jacket potatoes are always available, as well as cottage pie and chips. There is a family room and in summer the garden at the back is open. The opening hours are from 10.30 am to 3.30 pm and 6.30 pm to 11 pm. On Fridays and Saturdays the inn stays open in the afternoon. Sunday opening is 12 noon to 3 pm and 7 pm to 10.30 pm. Bar food is available from 12 noon to 2 pm.

Telephone: 01929 552503.

*How to get there:* Wareham is on the A351 between Poole and Corfe Castle. Wareham station is on the Waterloo—Weymouth line. The King's Arms is in North Street.

*Parking:* There are three car parks in the town centre.

*Length of the walk:* 3¹/₄ miles. Map: OS Landranger 195 Bournemouth and Purbeck (inn GR 922876).

*The beginning of the walk is up the main street to Wareham's most famous church, associated with Lawrence of Arabia. The town walls provide a view across the Piddle on the way to the edge of Poole Harbour. The path back is near the river Frome, with the tower of the main church as a guide.*

## The Walk

Turn left out of the King's Arms but cross the road well before reaching St Martin's. The pavement on the right side leads directly up to the Saxon church. Inside are impressive wall paintings and a Norman north aisle containing Eric Kennington's effigy of Lawrence of Arabia, intended for Westminster Abbey.

Go up the side of the church, to follow a path to St Martin's Lane. Turn left and right to go up onto the earth walls, where there is a view down to the river Piddle. The Saxon earth walls, once faced with stone, were cut down to half their original height by the Cromwellians to punish the town for supporting Charles I. Bear south with the wall until the ground dips for the Bell's Orchard Lane link path. Go left from the wall and cross a lane to go up a concrete path. After a stile by a gate the way is rough.

This is an old track running in an almost straight line through farmland down to the edge of Poole Harbour. Ignore a stile on the left – the way ahead is a permissive path. The path bends slightly at the tumbled buildings of Swineham Farm. At the far end go over a stile into an enclosed area. This is near the silted-up edge of Poole Harbour and there are often a few boats in the reeds. Roman pottery has been found here in the mud. Go over the second stile ahead and after a few yards the path turns right to run along the edge of the harbour. There is a brief view of the river Piddle flowing into the main waters. Also from the narrow path, occasionally enclosed by whitethorn and gorse,

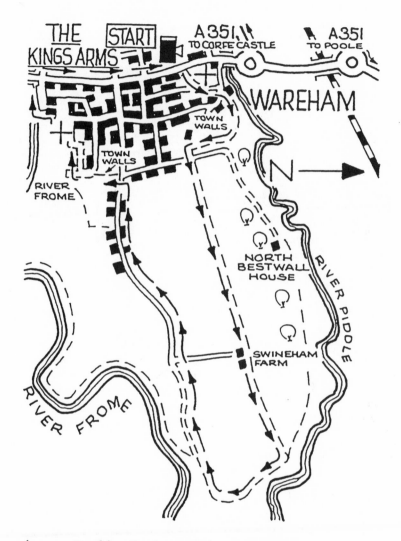

can be seen Rockley Sands, opposite, near Hamworthy. South are the Purbeck Hills.

When the path turns sharply west there is a view of Lady St Mary's church tower. The path is near the river Frome but, as it swings out to follow the river channel, drop down onto the rough lane (right) to continue west. From Swineham Farm the way becomes metalled and later is lined by houses. On reaching

*Wareham Channel.*

the town walls go left, up onto the 'East Walls' where there is a view of the church. The path runs down to join a lane. Turn right.

Lady St Mary church was rebuilt in 1842, on the site of a Saxon building, but contains much ancient stone work, as well as St Edward's Chapel, where the body of St Edward the Martyr, murdered at Corfe Castle in AD 979, was probably buried for three years before being moved to Shaftesbury Abbey – hence the two dates in the calendar for his feast day (18 March) and translation (20 June). The font is England's only hexagonal lead example and the huge east window is a memorial to John Hutchings, the famous 18th-century rector and historian.

This was once a monastic church and next door are the former domestic buildings of the Carthusian Priory, which has become a hotel. Earlier, from the 12th to early 15th century, when Wareham was an important port, the priory had been a cell of Lire Abbey in Normandy.

Cross Church Green to a narrow passage leading to The Quay by South Bridge where there is a view of a house standing on the castle mound. Just over the road is Abbot's Quay, where

Sherborne Abbey once kept a barn for storing shipments ready to go up the river Frome. Turn right up South Street to pass the early 18th-century manor house opposite the Black Bear. The Town Hall on the corner was designed by Thomas Hardy's first employer, Thomas Crickmay. On the opposite corner is the Red Lion, which the future Edward VII visited, incognito, as a 15 year old boy when exploring the town walls.

Continue up North Street to pass the solicitor's office on the corner of Cow Lane, where a plaque recalls that here Dinah Maria Craik wrote *John Halifax, Gentleman* in 1875. A short distance further on is the King's Arms.

# 14 Coldharbour
## The Silent Woman

This lonely building, set back from the roadside and opposite a milestone in Wareham Forest, started out as a cottage on a far flung corner of Lord Wimborne's Canford estate. The name is less certain for although a silent woman is usually said to refer to a beheaded saint there is a local suggestion that here the female figure is a former landlady who had her tongue cut out because smugglers feared she would gossip in Wareham market. When first a pub, the partly 18th century house was called the Angel but Thomas Hardy calls it 'The Quiet Woman Inn' in his novel *The Return of The Native*.

This spot in the forest is known as Coldharbour, which means 'refuge from the cold'. Appropriately, the Silent Woman has a log fire in winter and a cosy family room. In summer visitors sit outside at picnic tables and children enjoy the garden's play area, which has swings and a trampoline. This is a Hall & Woodhouse pub, so the two bars are stocked with Badger beers, including real ale Badger Best and Tanglefoot. The food specialities are

salad, home-made pies and curry. The BLT has smoked bacon. The ploughman's lunches feature Cheddar, matured Stilton and ham. Children can have a half ploughman's or a jumbo sausage with chips. Early arrivals can have morning coffee. The times of opening are, Monday to Saturday, 11 am to 2.30 pm and 6.30 pm to 11.30 pm. On Sunday the hours are 12 noon to 3 pm and 7 pm to 10.30 pm.
Telephone: 01929 552909.

*How to get there:* The Silent Woman at Coldharbour is 2 miles north-west of Wareham on the Wareham to Bere Regis road, which links the A351 to the A35.

*Parking:* There is a car park at the inn.

*Length of the walk:* 2 miles. Map: OS Landranger 195 Bournemouth and Purbeck (inn GR 902897).

*When Thomas Hardy knew the inn it stood on Dorset heathland, which he called 'Egdon Heath' in his books. Now much of this*

*Morden Bog in Wareham Forest.*

*heather and gorse is covered by Forestry Commission trees. The walk cuts through the dark forest to find some remaining heathland in the form of Morden Bog. Look out for the sika deer, who like marshy areas.*

## The Walk

From the pub turn left and cross the road to enter the wood. A disc on a post says 'Walkers Welcome Here'. Follow the main path ahead between the wood on the right and farmland on the left. The path runs past a main turning and downhill on the forest edge to a second right turning by a barn.

Go right here along the wide, straight path running through the tall trees. At a forest crossroads there are bat and bird boxes high up on the trees. Six species of bat are found here and resident birds include the tawny owl and woodpecker. Keep forward to the T-junction at the far end, where there is the Parson's Pleasure cairn – in memory of a former chief forester.

Turn right and soon young trees and a fringe of heather to the left gives way to the fragment of peat bog which forms part of Morden Bog. Beyond another junction the path crosses a stream, which flows from along a belt of hardwood trees. The path runs up to a viewpoint over the bogland before bearing round to the right. Soon the way passes a steep hill turning to the left. (Only for a good view go up here and turn left.)

Stay on the main path, which is crossed by brown and red waymarked routes, to reach the forest depot and office. Go ahead through the gate to the Wareham to Bere Regis road and turn right down the wide grass verge. A path becomes visible and at the bottom of the slope bears left to the road by another forest entrance. A few yards ahead is the Silent Woman.

# 15  Lytchett Minster
## The St Peter's Finger

Lytchett Minster is a village on the edge of a Poole Harbour inlet. The port of Poole was once reached by ferry from here. The 'Minster' may not be the church seen on this walk but the mother church at Lytchett Matravers, to the north. The St Peter's Finger stands at a crucial bend in the road – when the Southampton–Weymouth coach and four appeared round the corner the inn's ostler would sound a long post-horn and get ready to change the horses. There may have been a pub here in Tudor times but the present name is first recorded in 1755. The inn sign has always shown St Peter holding up his finger, although the name is a corruption of St Peter ad Vincula meaning 'St Peter in chains'. In Rome the church of St Peter in Chains contains the chains worn by the Apostle in prison just before his execution. Here in Lytchett tenants paid their rents on St Peter's Day until as recently as 1950. Strangely, the dedication of the village church which dates from medieval times is unknown.

The pub has a miniature set of chains blessed by the Pope, but the main theme is drums, with many on display from a disbanded Royal Artillery band. There are also examples of the buttons once made by villagers and sold at the Old Button Shop opposite. Children are welcome in the Chay Blyth suite behind the old building. In summer families sit at the tables in the back garden, where there is a swing and a slide as well as a dovecote, which always seems to have several doves popping in and out. There is even a children's toilet at the side and more seats across the lane by the pound if you want to look at the inn's famous frontage.

This is a Hall & Woodhouse house, so there are plenty of the local Blandford ales available. The menu is very long and includes lasagne and salads. As the pub is near Poole Harbour there are several fish dishes and a mixed seafood platter. A speciality is 'Prawns The Finger Way' – grilled prawns and cheese on granary bread. The St Peter's Finger is open from 11 am to 2.30 pm (3 pm on Saturday) and 6 pm to 11 pm. On Sunday the hours are 12 noon to 3 pm and 7 pm to 10.30 pm.

Telephone: 01202 622275.

*How to get there:* Lytchett Minster is at the beginning of the B3067, just off the A35 near Poole. The St Peter's Finger is on the right at the first bend in the village street when approaching from the west.

*Parking:* There is a car park behind the inn.

*Length of the walk:* 3 miles (shorter option available). Map: OS Landranger 195 Bournemouth and Purbeck (inn GR 961929).

*The walk has a view of the Purbeck Hills and is partly in woods before returning down the drive of the manor house. The figure of eight route allows for a very short walk for anyone wanting only a church visit and a single field to cross.*

## The Walk
Turn right out of the front of the St Peter's Finger to pass the garage and village shop and reach the church near the gates of South Lytchett Manor. Turn left up a footpath running between the churchyard and the school. The churchyard can be entered beyond the church tower, which is the oldest part

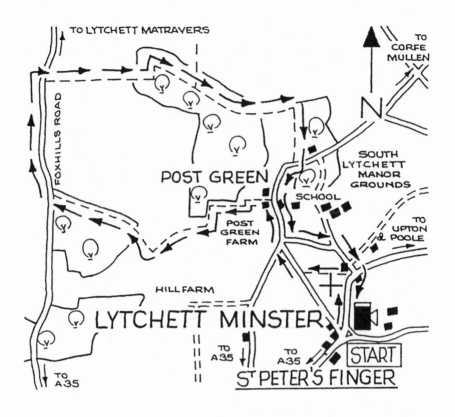

of the building. Outside, you can see the family tomb of the Lees family who hold the lordship of the manor. Nearby is explorer Sir Francis Younghusband's stone, which depicts the Dalai Lama's monastic palace. Cross the stile and go ahead over a field to another stile. Turn right up the lane to a crossroads.

*For the short-cut*, you can turn right here to follow the last section of the route back to the pub. The directions are in the last paragraph.

*For the main walk*, continue ahead to Post Green. The house on the right, built in 1748 by a Poole merchant, has been the Lees family residence since the manor house became a school in 1957.

Continue past Post Green Farm and turn left over a stile by a gate, just before the last house. Follow the hedged way to the end and climb over a stile on the left. At once turn right to go over another stile. Now hug the field boundary round three corners to reach a track by a gate. Turn right through the gate and walk down the track ahead to a stile by a gate. Beyond here do not be tempted to follow the main tread up the centre of the large field. Instead, keep left by the hedge to find, in the corner of the field, a stile leading to a wood.

The woodland path runs over two footbridges on its way uphill through the trees. Soon the way is level and just inside the wood. At a gate go right up a metalled lane known as Foxhills Road.

After ¼ mile leave the road to go right along a wooded path marked 'Stonard'. After some distance there is a double bend and the way widens to run below a bank of trees. Later the path rises to run round two sides of a field. Here, in addition to blackberries, there are wild raspberries. Just beyond a gate, the path meets a road.

Turn right to follow the road through Post Green. Rather than retracing the outward route through the churchyard turn left at the road junction.

At the next junction go right to join the drive from the manor house. This meets another estate road (which was the main road until the parkland was extended in 1907). Go right through the main gateway to follow the present main road to the St Peter's Finger.

*Dovecote in the garden of St Peter's Finger.*

# 16 Studland
## The Bankes Arms Hotel

In the last century this was called the Duke of Wellington, but eventually it took the name of the Bankes family of Kingston Lacey near Wimborne, who also owned Studland. Here they had a seaside villa, which survives as the nearby Manor House Hotel. The Bankes Arms, two Purbeck stone cottages, now belongs to the National Trust, which inherited much of the property in the area when the family died out in 1982.

This is a very popular pub in the summer and serves a huge number of ales, such as Marston's Pedigree, Poole Bosun, Brakspear, Fremlins, Wadworth 6X, Wethered Winter Royal, Flowers Original, Strong Country and Pompey Royal. There is an ever changing menu chalked up on a blackboard. Soup, garlic pâté, ploughman's lunches, filled jacket potatoes and salads usually feature. You will always find plenty of fish, such as grilled sardines, prawns, squid rings and sometimes local plaice and crab appears on the board. Children have their own menu and there is a family room. All food ordered at the bar can be brought to the tables in the field opposite, which has a good view of the bay. In winter log fires warm up returning walkers. Cream teas are available when there is all day opening.

The Bankes Arms is open from 11 am to 3 pm and 6.30 pm to 11 pm, except on Saturday when the pub is open all day. In summer the inn is open from 10.30 am to 11 pm, with food served from 12 noon to 2.30 pm and 7 pm to 9.30 pm. On Sunday the hours are 12 noon to 3 pm and 7 pm to 10.30 pm.

Telephone 01929 44225.

*How to get there:* Studland is on the B3351 Corfe Castle to Sandbanks Ferry road, which is a toll road north of the village. The Bankes Arms Hotel is on the east side of the village, next to the signed car park.

*Parking:* There is a National Trust car park next to the inn.

*Length of the walk:* 4 miles. Map: OS Landranger 195 Bournemouth and Purbeck (inn GR 038825).

*This is walking country and part of this route is the Dorset Coast Path. Even those not wishing to undertake the full circuit may want to go as far as Old Harry Rocks for the view, which is even better than the one from the Bankes Arms. The reward for continuing on the walk is a panoramic view from Ballard Down across Poole Harbour and Poole Bay to Bournemouth and over Swanage Bay to Durlston Castle.*

**The Walk**
On leaving the Bankes Arms go right downhill to a corner where there are two handy maps on a wall. Here turn left up a sheltered, stony path. After the entrance to a clifftop house the path continues through a small gate and along the boundary of the garden. At a junction of paths keep ahead and soon there is a view down into Studland Bay.

Continue ahead on the path, which now runs straight, and so is for a time away from the cliff edge, to pass through the

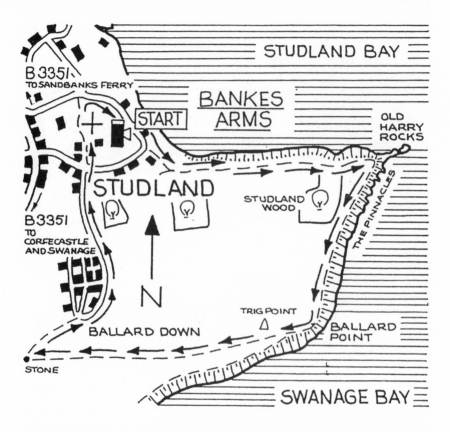

hazel Studland Wood. Beyond the trees the path runs onto the downland. Ahead are the Old Harry Rocks. Here, at the viewpoint, clear weather allows a view north to Bournemouth in Poole Bay and eastwards to the Isle of Wight.

The walk turns south with the cliff, which begins a gentle ascent. It is worth looking back occasionally at the sweep of ground and view. Continuing uphill you will find a double path – walkers on this National Trust land are now following the wider grass way a little back from the cliff edge.

Soon there is a view down onto The Pinnacle, with Peveril Point on the tip of Swanage Bay visible. Beyond is the castle at Durlston Head. This view improves dramatically and soon there is a fence to the right. When this fence turns right inland you should also turn right, leaving the coast path to run ahead.

*Old Harry Rocks.*

Stay by the fence to walk up the hill to the top of Ballard Down. Bear slightly right to the trig point, where there is a magnificent view down onto Poole Harbour on the right and Swanage on the left.

Continue ahead along the top of Ballard Down, with the views still on both sides. You may see smoke from a steam engine on the Swanage steam railway or even hear the engine's whistle. Just beyond a gate there are two ancient burial mounds to the left. The way is still ahead but gently uphill to a junction of paths at a lonely and redundant stile. Go right through a wooden gate (by a larger gate) to find the Rest And Be Thankful Stone, placed here in 1852 for those who come up the hill.

From the stone the path runs half-right over the field and downhill, where it acquires a stony surface. At a gateway go ahead to join a metalled lane. Follow this quiet road downhill past the line of dwellings. At the bottom the path turns right through a farmyard to reach Studland's village cross, which was restored in 1976. Look for the modern features, such as Concorde, in the carving.

Go ahead up to the churchyard. In front of you is the tomb of William Lawrence, landlord of the Bankes Arms from 1844 to 1869, when it was known as The Duke of Wellington – Lawrence's commander at the battle of Waterloo. Keep forward along the west end of the church and turn right down the far side to a kissing gate. Cross the field to a lane and go right for the Bankes Arms.

# 17 Horton
## Drusilla's

The building was a farmhouse in 1685 when the Duke of Monmouth is said to have sought food and shelter following defeat at the battle of Sedgemoor. He was arrested nearby shortly afterwards and later executed at the Tower of London. The splendid inn sign depicting German goosewoman Drusilla, with her flowing locks and geese, only went up in the early 90s, although the pub opened in 1978. From 1949 the thatched house had been Drusilla's Cottage tearoom and cream teas continue to be available on summer Saturdays. The round, thatched dining room has been added since the change to pub status, although in summer many people sit on the front terrace where there is a view of Horton Tower. From its first days as a pub there has been a welcome for children and there is a games room where families can eat and an outdoor children's play area.

Now Boddingtons, Flowers Original and Marston's Pedigree real ales are always available, along with one guest ale. The menu is extensive and all food ordered at the bar is brought to your table. The baguettes include a BLTM – bacon, lettuce, tomato and mayonnaise. Drusilla's is noted for its fish dishes, such as fish bake mornay and home-breaded plaice fillets served with salad or chips. There are always at least three vegetarian dishes and Dorset apple cake, among a long list of puddings. Children can choose from their own menu.

The times of opening are Monday to Friday from 11 am to 3 pm and 5.30 pm to 11 pm (open all afternoon on Saturday in summer). Sunday opening times are noon to 2 pm and 7 pm to 10.30 pm. Food is available from noon to 2 pm and until 9.30 pm in the evening.

Telephone: 01258 840297.

*How to get there:* Horton is off the B3078 Wimborne Minster to Cranborne road at Horton Inn, 6 miles north of Wimborne. The inn is just beyond the east end of the village.

*Parking:* There is plenty of room to park behind the inn.

*Length of the walk:* 2 miles. Map: OS Landranger 195 Bournemouth and Purbeck (inn GR 039075).

*Horton is well known for its 140 ft tower, built in 1726 by landowner Humphrey Sturt. Although called Sturt's Folly, it was intended as an observation post for watching deer movement. Early in the 20th century it lost its cupola and appeared forgotten until in the final decade the hilltop landmark was restored as a transmitting station for the Vodaphone network. The only occupants are owls. This walk goes to the base of the intriguing hexagon, where there is a view down onto Horton village, which has the only church dedicated to St Wolfreda and the county's largest vineyard.*

**The Walk**
From the inn turn right to walk towards the village at the bottom of the hill. You should always face on-coming traffic, but soon there is a wide grass verge on the left. Go as far as the junction at the bottom of the hill, where there is a white cottage. Just before the signpost go left over a stile and at once bear half-right across the corner of the field to another stile. Now keep half-left to a gate

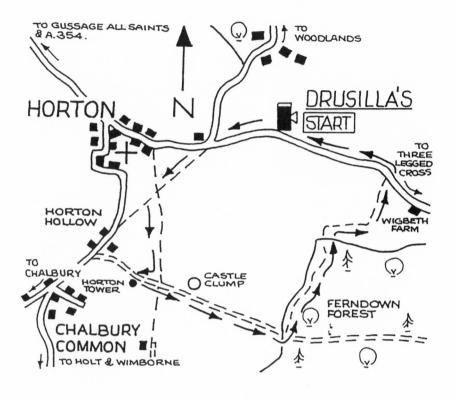

in the centre of the far side below the tower. Over to the right is Horton village.

Go over the fixed gate and stile. The path runs uphill, heading for a point just to the left of the tower. (There may be electric cattle fences but crossing points are indicated.) As the view improves, continue up across the sloping field to the far top left corner.

Climb over the stile and turn right along the track for a close look at the tower. Here there is a bird's eye view of Horton and the 11-acre vineyard behind the village. After enjoying the view retrace your steps to the stile and go through the gate.

Follow the track, which passes Castle Clump (no trees) before running gently downhill to a gate on the edge of Ferndown Forest. After a few yards go left along a narrow path, which becomes dark as it runs through the mixed trees. At the far end go left to a stile. Continue to the right, round the corner, to go over another stile.

81

*Horton Tower.*

Stay by the right-hand field boundary to go ahead and round a corner. At once bear half-left to cut the next field corner and find two stiles in the thick boundary hedge.

Having crossed the stiles, turn left up another field. Here there is a view over to Wigbeth Farm, which is famous for its sausage shop. Callers are welcome via the road entrance from 9.30 am to 5 pm, except Wednesday and Sunday (telephone: 01258 840723).

Beyond a stile go left along the road (walking on the right-hand side) to find Drusilla's, round the corner.

# ⑱ Woolsbridge
# The Old Barn Farm

Old Barn Farm does not call itself an inn and instead sticks to its old name, for this was a dairy farm belonging to Lord Normanton whose family seat is Somerley on the far side of Ringwood forest. Today the thatched building has an attractive dining room extension beneath a dovecote and the milking shed has become a skittle alley. Outside there is a pond with a footbridge approach to the front door. This is a place which makes children feel most welcome. A play area at the front has a slide and hidden at the back there is a children's fun tree.

The pub, which is the old farmhouse, is a Bass house with Ruddles County and Wadworth 6X. There are always at least two real ales available. Even tap water is happily offered to those who prefer it to the sparkling variety and this homely touch is reflected in the food. The ploughman's lunches, which all come with an apple for 'pudding', include Old Barn Special, featuring ham and cheese in the farmhouse tradition. The various versions of the Old Barn Mixed Grill include a steak. There are always vegetarian dishes. The children's menu offers burgers, fish fingers and jumbo sausage. There are two family tables inside for those having the bar food and in summer you will find tables with sun umbrellas on the lawn outside. The times of opening are 11 am to 3 pm and 6 pm to 11 pm. On Sundays the evening hours are 7 pm to 10.30 pm.

Telephone: 01202 824925.

*How to get there:* Woolsbridge lies on the Ashley Heath to Three Legged Cross road, off the A31 between Wimborne Minster and Ringwood. The inn is west of the well-signed entrance to Moors Valley country park.

*Parking:* There is a car park at the inn.

*Length of the walk:* 2½ miles. Map: OS Landranger 195 Bournemouth and Purbeck (inn GR 097049).

*The walk is across the flat Lower Common beside Ringwood Forest, which is Dorset's barrier along its border with Hampshire.*

*The Moors Valley Railway.*

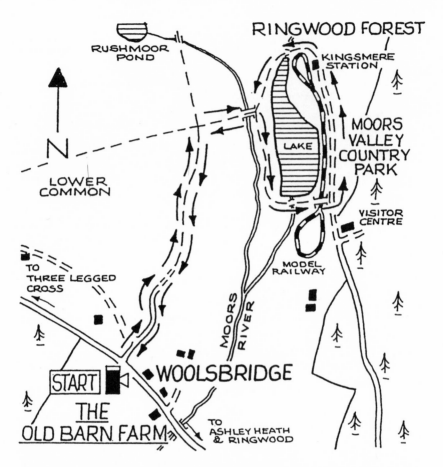

*The open, almost treeless, land on the west side is mostly used as horse paddocks but there is a surprise grass airfield for model aircraft. The route continues around the lake at Moors Valley, which attracts migratory birds and has an impressive steam railway (telephone: 01425 471415) running alongside.*

**The Walk**

Go right from the inn for a few yards to turn up a metalled lane, marked 'Ashley Heath Industrial Estate' and 'Homeacres Farmhouse'. The many signs include a small, blue, footpath waymark. Soon there is a large field to the left. After a double bend the road is more a path as it runs through a gateway. After a banger racing circuit and another double bend the path passes through a field used for regular model aircraft flights. Continue ahead to a junction of paths.

Turn right and follow a wooded path leading to a gate with a stile. Keep ahead over the wooden and brick bridges of the Moors river, which flows from nearby Rushmoor Pond to join the river Stour behind Bournemouth.

Ahead is Moors Lake, which was constructed in the early 1980s as a flood control to hold water back after heavy rainfall. Go right to follow the path round to the level crossing at Lakeside. Cross the line, using the footbridge.

There is a Visitor Centre a short distance to the right, but the walk continues to the left, along the road which follows the railway line to Kingsmere station, which until 1985 was King's farm. Now steam trains are timetabled every weekend (daily in summer) on the $7^1/_4''$ gauge track which runs for $1^1/_2$ miles. On this working railway even the ice–cream on sale at the stations is delivered by rail, in an insulated van.

Continue round the rear of the station to complete the circuit of the lake and retrace the outward route. The way back is to the right over the Moors river and along the wooded path. Once in the open go ahead for a few yards to turn left. Follow this path all the way back to the main road and go right for Old Barn Farm.

# 19 Wallisdown
# The Dorset Knob

Artist Paul Nash described Dorset knobs as 'very light rusks about the size and shape of golf balls, with the resilience of a ship's biscuit', adding that 'they go very well with Blue Vinny Cheese'. Others dip them in tea. The knobs may have originated in medieval times, but today they are only made by Moores of Morcombelake, near Bridport, whose knob packet appears on the pub sign.

Inside this Poole suburb pub there is one large lounge bar, decorated with horse brasses, cartoons of local characters and old bank notes. Appropriately, this friendly Dorset pub is a Hall & Woodhouse inn with their Dorset ales available. A ploughman's lunch here can be Dorset knobs with Cheddar or Stilton rather than the bread version. Soup, pâté with toast and steak and kidney pie are also always on the menu. The special on the board is sometimes vegetarian cannelloni and crusty bread. The Dorset Knob is open from 11 am to 11 pm on Monday to Saturday. On Sunday the opening hours are 12 noon to 3 pm and 7 pm to

10.30 pm. Food is always available between 12 noon and 3 pm, and in the evening there are usually rolls or knobs.

Telephone: 01202 748427.

*How to get there:* The pub, on the south side of Wallisdown, is on the A3040, Alder Road, linking Wallisdown with Branksome. You will find it in the valley just south of the Sainsbury's roundabout.

*Parking:* There is a car park at the inn.

*Length of the walk:* 2 miles. Map: OS Landranger 195 Bournemouth and Purbeck (inn GR 060962).

*Although not immediately apparent, the pub stands on heathland and a few yards behind is an example of preserved heath, providing a haven for snakes, butterflies and 16 species of dragonfly. The walk goes over a hill onto Talbot Heath, which is bisected by the infant river Bourne on its way to Bournemouth. The purple heather here gives an idea of the Dorset heathland known to Thomas Hardy in the 19th century.*

## The Walk

Turn right out of the pub to pass the garage and go right again into Sharp Road. Walk to the end to enter the Alder Hills nature reserve. Go left and soon the way is up sandy steps to a viewpoint over a lake.

Avoid the steps to the left and continue ahead. (The windowless brick building to the left is Sainsbury's.) Where the fence turns sharp left to run up to garages, go ahead to head for the pylon. There is a narrow path in the heather. Go over the brow and down steps. The path winds down and up to a reserve entrance by the pylon.

Walk round to the front of the houses and turn left. Take the **second** turning on the right, marked 'Franham Road 58–108'. There is a view down on to Talbot Heath's woods, farm and heathland. At the end of the road keep ahead on the footpath to reach another road. Cross over to go down Merrow Avenue, almost opposite. After a short distance, and just before the bend, go down a short unmarked road on the left leading to garages.

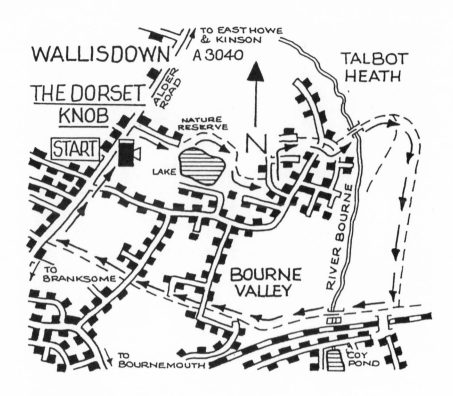

Continue across the grass on the track. To the right there is a distant view of the spire of St John's church (Surrey Road), which stands just inside the old Dorset boundary.

Keep ahead into the trees to cross the Bourne stream, which has flowed down Bourne Bottom from Canford Heath. Continue forward on a path which bends to the right. Keep left where there is a divide, to go uphill onto open heath. The path appears to be heading to the left of the two masts – although later it is found to be running to the right.

At the top of the hill there is a panoramic view down into the valley. Continue ahead through trees, where there is briefly a view behind of Talbot Village church tower. This is a model village planned in 1850 by Georgina Talbot, who gave her name to the area.

On reaching a T-junction go right, along a path by the railway. After a bridge, the path quickly falls as the railway runs along an

*Path over Talbot Heath.*

embankment. At the bottom a footbridge carries the path across the Bourne, just before it flows under the railway embankment, which was constructed in 1886. The stream feeds Coy Pond on the other side, before joining the other arm of the Bourne in the rural Upper Pleasure Gardens.

The way now climbs out of the valley. After crossing the end of a road, the path is straight and often wooded for 1/2 mile as it runs up and down and across two roads. At the far end there is Alder Road. Turn right along the main road to find the Dorset Knob at the bottom of the hill.

# 20 Mudeford
# The Haven House Inn

The Haven House Inn is on the exposed tip of the quay at the entrance to Christchurch Harbour, which can be idyllic in summer and bracing in winter. Although picturesque, this is a working quay with fishing boats and a ferry as well as small launches for holidaymakers from nearby beaches. There has been an inn here for about 300 years. In 1784 a cannon ball from a naval sloop hit the roof during the so-called battle of Mudeford, when customs men ambushed smugglers. As a result the body of a hanged smuggler was exhibited outside the inn.

The smugglers may have gone but there are still full-time fishermen to be found at the stone-floored pub, which has a tiny entrance facing away from the strong sea gales. This is a freehouse, stocking Devenish ales (it was once a Devenish house), Whitbread, Wadworth 6X, Bentley's Yorkshire Bitter and Boddingtons. The pub is small but it has a large kitchen offering plenty of fish – much of it landed just outside. There is fisherman's pie and fishy sandwiches. Prawns are still ordered by the pint and come with seafood dip and brown buttered bread. For children there is cod, peas and chips. Families eat in the Haven Café, which shares the inn kitchen and has, unlike the original pub, a view of the fast-flowing harbour run beyond the inevitable pile of lobster pots. Next door, fresh fish is on sale to take home. The Haven House Inn is open from 11 am to 3 pm and 6 pm to 11 pm but the Haven Café remains open all afternoon. On Sunday the hours are 12 noon to 3 pm and 7 pm to 10.30 pm.

Telephone: 01425 272609.

*How to get there:* Mudeford is signposted from Purewell in Christchurch on the A35. In summer it can be reached by ferry from the beach behind Hengistbury Head.

*Parking:* There is a public car park on the Haven next to the inn.

*Length of the walk:* 3¹/₂ miles (a short-cut, leaving out Highcliffe Castle, is possible). Map: OS Landranger 195 Bournemouth and Purbeck (inn GR 183916).

*This walk follows the rising cliff up to viewpoint woodland, before passing through the grounds of the extraordinary Highcliffe Castle, built on a spot described in the 1820s as 'having one of the most beautiful views in the kingdom'.*

## The Walk

Walk along the waterside by the harbour entrance. Beyond the car park there is a path running in front of Sandhills' garden, now used for holiday caravans. George III and Admiral Nelson both visited the house. Guests at the small end house, Gundimore, have included poets Coleridge, Southey and Walter Scott, who wrote *Marmion* here.

On meeting a road continue along the coast, just inland of the Avon Beach car park. A footpath runs up to the top of the low cliff and under the line of trees. Look out for the thatched house. Where the parallel road turns inland go ahead down the slope to join a promenade. At the end of the line of beach huts go round the back to go up onto the low cliff at Steamer Point – so called after a beached steamer which was used as a beach hut by the

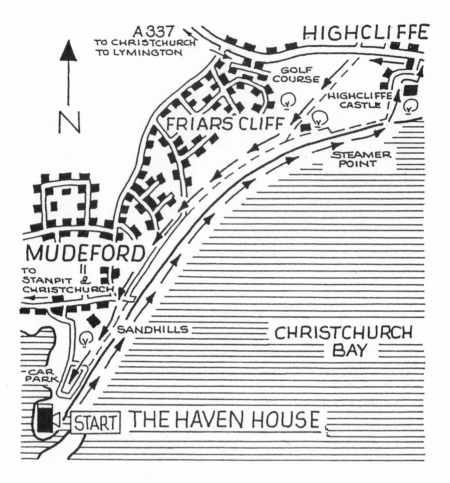

Highcliffe Castle residents.

Walk past the Boardsailing Club to find a gate leading to Steamer Point woodland. Go through the pedestrian entrance and up the clifftop path, which runs past the Coastguard Training Centre and up to a Woodland Wildlife Centre. The building has a fine view back into the harbour and information on the wildlife in Steamer Point Woods. Look carefully at the nature mural and find the drawers which open.

Continue into the woodland and, where the way divides, go right. Behind the first building descend the steps to the beach.

On the beach you can turn right back to the inn, if you wish.